VOICES
OF ADULT
LEARNERS

VOICES OF ADULT LEARNERS

24th Edition—2020

A Virginia Festival of the Book Event

TJACE@PVCC is an adult education program serving Albemarle, Fluvanna, Greene, Louisa, and Nelson Counties and the City of Charlottesville.

Carol Coffey, Director, TJACE@PVCC
ccoffey@pvcc.edu

For a complete listing of stories go to:
www.pvcc.edu/tjace

For information about the Virginia Festival of the Book, go to:
www.vabook.org

Cover and interior design: Lisa Zoë Willow
Cover image: pixabay.com
Section Photos: Chip King

Contents

Work   41

Education   55

Preface

"I left behind old pillows of borrowed beds of my past loneliness as a foreigner in my new home in Virginia. Reading, writing, and speaking English taught me how education changes each of our lives for the better." —*Xueping Wang*

"There is no better education than what life teaches you." —*Ofelia Abundio Alonso*

"I started thinking back to those days that everybody was telling me, "you can't." After that I made some changes inside me, that no one can tell me who I am and what I am capable of."
—*Seyed Ali Hashemi*

Stories from our 2020 VOICES winners remind us of the importance of lifelong learning: Education comes from organized instruction and random life experiences. Learning comes from self-reflection, internal awareness and reckoning. Success comes from hard work and action. The power of trust, kindness and love can lead to deep transformational change.

These stories demonstrate why adult education and literacy programs matter and must continue to exist. We believe it is important to honor adult learners, and it is equally important for their VOICES to be heard. TJACE@PVCC is proud to sponsor VOICES of Adult Learners and share this gift with you.

Thank you, wise writers (and your teachers/tutors)

for inspiring us to embrace our own lifelong learning moments and perhaps "heel the world." Soo Lim

Carol Coffey,
Director, TJACE@PVCC

Acknowledgments

The work and generosity of many individuals combined to make Voices of Adult Learners an important program.

Our judges, Meredith Dickens, Harriet Kuhr, Mitzi Ware, and Juandiego Wade thoughtfully read and selected the stories for this publication.

Thanks to our partners for this event—Literacy Volunteers of Charlottesville Albemarle. www.literacy-forall.org

Thanks to the Virginia Foundation for the Humanities and the Virginia Festival of the Book for their continued support.

For information on how you can support area adult education and literacy programs or register for classes, please call 434-961-5461 or visit www.pvcc.edu/tjace.

Family

My Promise

By Enrique Velazguez

Everyone thinks that the life of poor children is easy. But my life when I was only one boy was not to be easy. My dad struggled to pay for everything for my brothers, my sister, and me. He worked construction. He didn't earn much money. My mom helped him by washing and ironing clothes. I think it was so much pressure for them. For this reason, we had to work when we were only children.

But thanks to our parents, we are now adults, and good people. We really like to work. Today, I still see my mom when she said that we did not have anything to eat. That made me sad because I was only one little boy, and I had not helped with much. Always she told me to search how to get ahead. She is the best mom in the world!

And my promise now, when I am only one boy, is that my parents will never lack anything, because they always gave us what they could with love even, if it was not enough. Now thanks to all their support, I help them with everything I can.

I think now they don't need anything. I hope to help them. And someday I hope to return to them. I miss them a lot, but it is very hard for me because I have my little daughter. It is complicated to return to Mexico with her in my life. I love my daughter a lot. I don't want to leave her alone, because if I leave, I may not be able to return. I think my promise is happening but not as I would like. I hope to continue helping them and be with them someday.

Never leave those who gave you life, who gave all for you. Thanks to them you are who you are. Thanks to them, you can see a lot of things, you can smell and give love to those you love thanks to them you can touch one world different. Many know my name. They criticize me but they don't know my story. This is a fraction of me. It is part of my promise.

The Power of Love

By Wendy Zhou

Today I want to share a true story about a power. It is a love power, which pushes me forward all the time and has led me to become a better person. So I am grateful for the power of love.

First, I want to introduce my greatest love, a gentleman, who is my husband. He loves me deeply, and supports me in anything what I want to do. We fell in love in 2012, when he was a master's student. I was an administrate staff in our university. He was always in my mind when I led thirty students to participate in a social practice that summer in the Xinjiang province. This place was a very remote unsafety city. Even though I went there three times before, I still felt very tired and stressed. I needed to demonstrate outstanding performance and also insure the students' safety. It was very important, at that time, my new love told me, that I would be strong. He called me almost 20 times, and he waited for me until the morning always. He helped me solve a lot of problems. And when I came back to my hometown, he waited for me almost seven hours in the airport. He always ensured contact with me to know I was safe. So in the last four years, my job has been perfect due to the power of love.

Then I quit my job of five years to follow my love to a new city where he got a job. I decided to pursue my master's degree in that city. I knew that we would miss each other if we weren't in same city. Although I felt high pressure of my job, I chose to study for the master's test in my spare time. I studied every day until midnight. I kept it up 6 months, and finally I got my MBA admission letter. At this point, my love and I knew that we would be able to stay in the same city together, so we got married. We all know that studying for a master's test while you work is not an easy thing. It is a challenge for all people. To be frank, I want to give up when I feel stressed and tired, but I don't, because my husband together with me gives me power which makes me never give up. This is the power of love.

Recently, I came to Charlottesville. It is a very strange city for me, because my husband came here before me to start the study of his PHD. When he came here I felt he is not so good as the time I was in China. So I decided leave my country, leave my family, give up my job, give up all the things and people to come here to be with him. All this is the power of love.

At the beginning, I felt very lonely: no friends, no job, even a language barrier in this strange city. But now I think I have adapted to the environment and I try to do my best. Now we are having a baby, we will become a family of three people, we are having a happy life. All this is the power of love.

The Power of love lets me know what is the true life and tells me I am in control of my life. The Power of love makes me understand where I should go and shows me the directions. Also the Power of love teaches me how to change my self and achieve my life goal.

Thanks my love, love my lover forever.

Nothing Else Is Stronger Than a Family

By Robelina Bernardo

I would like to tell you about my story and my complicated family. I am the only child by my parents, but I was not raised by my parents. I was born in a small town in the Philippines, called Tagudin. My hometown was really a tiny place where everyone knows everything. There were not a lot of opportunities of work.

Six months after I was born, my mom left immediately for Italy. The reason why is because she was already living over there for years. She also had a good job. And it was impossible for her to take me and my dad with her at that time. So she had to leave me and my dad behind. But it didn't mean she never came to visit us. Instead she was coming back and forth from Italy to Philippines once a year. She would stay one month out of the year. Since my mom left me when I was just a baby, every time she came to visit us, she was a stranger to me. I remember that I was so mean to her because I didn't really know her very well. Of course, I now know it was hard for her, too.

My dad raised me for five years in the Philippines,

with the help of his parents, his sisters and also my mom's parents. But then he joined my mom in Italy to find a better job, and left me behind. Therefore, both of my parents left me behind, in the Philippines, with my aunties and grandparents. In those years, without my parents, I felt abandoned from the both of them. Even if they were doing it for a better future, I didn't understand it as a child. For that reason, my unusual childhood kind of affected me for who I am now. However, when I was nine years old, my mom decided that it was time to take me with them to Italy. I didn't even realize that I was moving, when all of a sudden I landed in another city, another country and another continent.

I arrived in my new city, Milan. It was a BIG change for me! Naturally, I was so sad to leave my aunties and my grandparents, who raised me. I was sad to leave behind friends. Leaving everything and everyone I knew was heartbreaking. But in the meantime I was excited and overwhelmed to start a new chapter. For me moving to Italy was like living in another planet. Everything was so different: the people, the place, the food, the culture and especially the language (so complicated!). In the beginning, certainly, it was pretty difficult. But, eventually, I've had to adapt, in some way, and grew up in this new country.

The strangest thing, was finally living with my parents. Honestly, I didn't know how to do that! It was so complicated living there especially with my mom since we've never lived together. I had to get to know her better and she was just doing the mom thing where I wasn't used to having a mother. Gradually, living together, we've learned so much about each other.

9

I learned to be a daughter and she learned to be a mother. All three of us, me, my dad and my mom, living in the same place, in the same home, we've learned to love each other in our own way. We became a great family.

Last Chance to Save Nature

By Alex Laheb

I am 21. My dream is to have a big family, many children and grandchildren and a huge house on top of a hill. I want to wake up every morning and hear the birds' songs, to see butterflies, bees and squirrels. I want to be surrounded by flowers and trees. I want to walk under the clean rain and not, when I'm older, acidic rain. But I think this is not realistic with the way of life that we are following. I have a feeling that we won't have such a beautiful life.

Today we are slowly killing the world and nature. We put in danger our children, our grandchildren and ourselves. And not only humans but all kinds of animals. A good example is Australia. We humans are responsible for the fires that killed billions of poor animals. It's all because we live too comfortably. But our children and grandchildren will pay for our selfishness. We still have a chance to change the future. Let's do something before it is too late.

Nasty Big Dog

By Justin Ngwapapo

I was born in 1972 in the Democratic of Congo, in the city of Kiri.

When I was nine years old, one day I went to draw water from the tap. When I was walking with my demi john (vase glass) full of water on my head, I saw a big dog coming with his handler. The dog handler was a person with a disability. I continued to walk on my way without looking left or right because I was afraid of the dog. While I was moving forward, suddenly the dog came and bit my leg. I cried and cried, but I did not stand up because I had to take care of the glass vase of water I carried. I did not want to break it also.

When I arrived back home, my parents were very angry. My father took me to show him where the dog bit me. We returned there and I showed my father the address. He angrily asked the dog handler about the dog bite. "I am very sorry sir, forgive me and my dog", said the dog handler. "Right now, what can you do to cure my son from this bite?" asked my father. "Let me do something," replied the dog owner.

He called his dog, stripped some dog hairs, mixed them with the dust of Tobacco (traditional) and rubbed in my injury. Curiously, two days later the dog bite was cured. It was a magic remedy that I have never seen. But unfortunately since then, I have a phobia of dogs. If I meet one on my way, I have to change my direction. In short, I like dogs, but who can help me overcome this phobia?

Life Doesn't Ask You if You Want to Be Strong. Life Teaches You to Be Strong

By Ofelia Abundio Alonso

My name is Ofelia Abundio Alonso. I am from San Miguel Xaltepec, Palmar de Bravo, Pue, Mexico. I am the oldest of nine siblings, six sisters and three brothers.

It is 2001. I am thirteen years old. Mom and Dad fought, and Mom has left home because Dad almost killed her. I have to leave middle school. Dad is drunk and has lost his senses. I am afraid and hate my dad for hurting my mom and making her leave. We have nothing to eat. We ask my dad for food, and he gives us hard, raw corn and beans. I am thirteen years old. I don't know what to do with my brothers and sisters. It is too much responsibility for me. I cry and pray to God that my mom comes home.

Eight days later, my mother comes home and forgives my father, and they are happy again. I am happy because my mom is home.

I am thirteen years old. I have to leave school because we don't have any money. My mother tells me to stay in school, but I know I need to work to help my family because my dad only works when he wants. I don't blame him because he grew up without a father to teach him how to be a man.

I start working at a farm six days a week, and I help my mother sell Pan de Burro, Elotes, Esquites, and Chicharrones on the weekend. During Lent, we sell fried fish and other snacks. To pay back a loan my father borrowed, my parents and I go to Baja California for six months to work, but my mother misses her children, so we go home.

When we get home, my mother tells me I have to get a job. My cousin finds me a job at a chicken farm. I work six days a week. I am fifteen years old. Each day I have to pick up forty-five cases of eggs. Each case holds three hundred and sixty-five eggs. The first day, I can't do it by myself, but my coworkers help me. They help me until I can do it by myself.

I hate this job. The hens poop everywhere. It smells terrible. My shoes are too old, so I have to walk barefoot. I get poop on my feet. Worms crawl in the poop and on my feet. There are rats. There are thousands of flies. I eat my lunch inside as quickly as I can, so I can keep working and finish as soon as possible. I can't enjoy my food. One by one, my sisters and my mother join me. We work at the chicken farm for three years. I hate this job.

One day I decide I can't take it anymore. I am afraid, because I know I need to work to help my family, but I can't watch my parents fight anymore. I have to escape. I am eighteen years old. I immigrate to the United States.

There is no better education than what life teaches you.

A Strong Soul—My Saving Grace

By Kayla Marie Morris

Well here is my story! Life was great growing up as a kid!! My parents were happily married. I had a younger brother who I always watched out for. When I turned 16 that's when I really started to notice things. My parents weren't as happy as I thought.

My dad was an alcoholic and he did a lot of drugs. It had gotten so bad that if my dad didn't have beer or drugs, he would abuse me, my brother, and my sisters. So, my Mom started cheating on my dad. She found her a boyfriend. When I first met him, he was really nice. Then one day my dad found out about him. That whole day he did nothing but take out his anger on me, my mom, and my siblings. That same day my mom finally told my dad, "It's over—leave!" So, my dad left. It honestly was a happy and sad day for me. After that my mom would have her boyfriend over almost every night. Well after them being together for a few months, he got my mom hooked on drugs. Through all of this I had the best boyfriend in the whole world!

We met at Subway. Collin stuck by my side through everything. Then I found out I was pregnant by him. My mom ended up going to jail for some bad stuff. Six months of my pregnancy all I had was my fiancé, his family, and my uncle. I ended up dropping out of school because of everything that happened with my mom and my pregnancy.

Then my saving grace Daniel Shane Coleman arrived,

my sweet, handsome baby boy—the little boy who had kept me pushing through everything: mom going to jail and my brother and sister going to foster care. Daniel kept me going through everything. Every night before I would go to bed, I would tell my son "I love you so much and I promise your life will be so much better than mine ever was."

Now my life is 100% better. When Daniel was about six months old, Collin and I moved into our own place. About four months later, I started going back to school. The main reason I'm going back to school is so I can do my dream job of becoming a photographer. I want to show my son that no matter what life throws at you, you can do any and everything you set your mind to. This is my story. This is how my son saved my life.

A Valiant Angel That Saved My Life

By Cindy Paola Rodriguez

I was 16 when the doctor told me "You are preg-nant!" I was terrified with the idea to be a mom; a bad mom! I was asking many questions to myself like: Now, what am I going to do? Is my baby going to be healthy? What is my baby going to look like? I drew almost 100 pages of a notebook with different baby faces that came to my mind. It was because I was extremely impatient thinking about how she was going to look like. I said "she" because I always knew that my first baby would be a beautiful girl that I was ready to name Valentina! Time flew and the big day came! She was born during the afternoon of a Friday on January 10th. I can still remember how hard the la-bor pain was.... However, it stopped just when I heard her crying but I remember that my body was com-pletely shocked and I could not take her in my arms. The nurse patiently said, "It is ok, Mom." Next, she took my daughter away from me to give her a bath and put some clothes on her. Later, I had the most fascinating experience in my life: even though at least ten babies were crying at the same time, I always knew the sound of her crying. After probably 20 to 30 minutes a nurse brought her to me, my girl. That light on her eyes lit up my entire life, I was feeling as if my soul was smiling.

We have many amazing stories together, now after 17 years, I know that my life without her probably would have ended a long time ago because I was a sad broken teenager. She saved me because she brought me hope, motivation, happiness and that feeling of "I can do everything." She gave me enough courage so, after being a teenage mother who had not even finished school, we completed not one but two college degrees. I even went to Madrid, Spain to study financial management! And I said, "we completed" because for her it was not easy to be the daughter of a busy and tired mom. More than a daughter, she has been an exceptional inspiration on this journey. Now, we are living in the USA and we both are learning English, of course. She is brave, gorgeous, clever, and generous. She has a wonderful sense of humor. She is doing an excellent job at her school. Also, she is a magnificent soccer player, salsa music dancer and makeup artist.

She is my daughter, Angely Valentina!

Where I Come From

A Moment That Lasts a Lifetime

By Keabetswe Leshoe

Bound by the Red Sea, the Mediterranean Sea, the Indian Ocean and the Atlantic Ocean lies the beautiful land of Africa. Many call it the Mother Land, some say it's that continent that looks like a question mark, and a few, including myself at some point, have considered its shape to be like that of a lopsided ice cream cone, with some scoops leaning heavily to the left. To me, it is the continent that carries my birthplace: South Africa.

With its great natural beauty, eleven official languages, rich natural resources, the only country in the world to include another country within its borders, a horizontal 'Y' shape on the flag which represents a once divided nation converging and working together in harmony, South Africa was given its nickname "Rainbow Nation" to acknowledge its attempts to create a semblance of unity, ('Ubuntu' Xhosa), 'Botho' (Sotho and Setswana), 'Vanhu' (Shona), 'Vhuthu" (Venda), 'Mensdom' (Afrikaans), in an ethnically diverse country after apartheid ended in 1994.

Born in a small town called Mahikeng, I started learning at a young age that you do not have to know someone to greet them. We refer to this as Ubuntu, a Xhosa word which translates to "I am because we are..." At first it did not make sense to me, but as time went on and I got older, I understood that in my culture, everyone is your mother, everyone is your father, everyone is your sister and everyone is your brother. I was to treat everyone, outside of the house I grew up in, with the same respect as those who lived outside of it.

Growing up, I had a lot of book smarts which a lot of my peers found to be a little more than they could handle. Because of my intelligence, it was hard to make friends. I felt alone, even though I was surrounded by a crowd of people every day. One Sunday afternoon, I noticed that my mother was going through the same thing as myself. Men and women that we attended church with would greet the ladies my mother was standing with, but not her. How she responded was inspiring to me.

She greeted them after they walked past her. Not sarcastically, but in the same manner she had greeted the ladies she was with. As we were in the car driving home, I asked her why she did that and she responded by saying "Madume ha a rekesiwe (saying hello does not cost anything; being kind and respectful does not cost anything), and no matter how people may treat you in life, always be respectful because that is how you were raised." I went back to school the next day, which was Monday of course, and that was the first day of the rest of my life where I eventually made new friends, lasting memories, and left a footprint at the school that many use as a stepping stool to this day: kindness is the best form of humanity.

That moment I shared with my mother has made me into the woman I am today. Because of that moment, I have been complimented on my kindness and my manners wherever I travelled, whether it was in China or here in Virginia and even back home in South Africa, and I thank my mother every day for that moment; a moment that lasts a lifetime.

My Heart Split

By Wenjin Wang

Wake up confused,
maybe from a bad dream, which I do not remember.
I do not even know where I am.

Too bright to keep my eyes open,
I guess I am in Kunming, China.

An early spring morning.
The sky is clear and blue,
cherry blossoms start to bloom,
thick pale pink reflected on my window.
My bedroom is rendered with pink too.

My grey-haired mother is waiting for me
downstairs, with a delicious hot meal,
and her never changed, 40-year-old beautiful
smile.

Oh, no!

I miss my home in Virginia, USA,
on a deep winter morning.
Out of my window, sun rises up from the east,
woods lit up in the opposite.
A boring grey and brown world turns into shining
golden palace, like in God's glory.

Dried knockout roses still sleeping on the branches,
new buds and blue birds are waiting for spring.

My precious daughter is running towards me,
hopping around like a rabbit,
giggling like a little girl, when she was
8 months old and called me mom for her first time.

Oh, no!
Literally I am in my Crozet home, Virginia.

My heart feels like it's split.
I love my home here,
I miss my mom yonder.

The New Bicycle

By Sahar Hashemi

When I was about seven years old, I loved to ride my bicycle. I used to ride a lot on my brother's bike. One day my parents my parents gifted me a bicycle and I cannot explain how happy I was that day. Finally, I had my own bicycle.

We decided to go to the park and have a picnic, so I could ride my bicycle. That park in Mashhad, Iran was very big. There were very huge trees all around and grassy fields. But there was not a special lane for bicycles so I could only ride in the lane that people used for walking and running. And that lane was crowded! I had to ring my bel to let people know I was coming through.

After eating dinner at the park, I said to my parents: "I'm going to ride my bicycle." "Don't go so far please I'll watch you," my mom said. And in a quick second I went off into the crowd. I was very happy that time. Every time that I pushed the pedal harder, the wind was playing harder with my hair. And I loved it very much. After about half an hour of riding, I decided to go back to my family. But suddenly, I realized that I didn't know where I was. "Where are you, mom? I can't see you." I said, with a very low voice. I was scared, nobody was there. There were only trees and the wind sound that came from inside the trees. Everyone in my family had left and it was dark. I was about to cry. I started walking to find someone to ask for help. After some time, I found a policeman. I ran to him and asked him to help me. He was very nice and started to talk to me to make me comfortable.

After half an hour I found my dad running around the park and I screamed, "Daddy!" He turned and saw me, and I started to cry. He ran to me and hugged me. My father thanked the policeman for helping me. That evening I promised myself that I would never go far from my parents again. But a week later, I was riding by myself again.

A Lost Coin

By Ezekiel Bizimana

I was born in DR Congo but I lived in Tanzania over twenty-three years. I left my parents in Congo when I was about seven years old. I came to Tanzania. When I first arrived in Tanzania, I had a hard time because the one who brought me left me on the sandy beach where passengers get off boats. He disappeared and I never saw him again. I fell sleep without eating. Starvation did not bother me because I was tired.

The next day I got up and went to the street to see if I could find anything to eat. As I went around I collected a coin I found on the ground. I was very happy! I kept going around the same area hoping I would find more coins. I didn't find any. I went to a nearby restaurant to get food but before I entered I wanted to make sure I still had money. I found my coin was lost. My pocket had a hole in it. I can't forget that day.

Someone saw me and asked me why I looked like I was sad. I told him I was angry because I had lost my money. This man took me and bought food for me. When we eat he asked me, "how often do you think about trust?" And he added, "can you tell me things that makes someone to be trustworthy?" I said, "I don't know." He said, "next time you need trust, even when you're down, believe and you will see another door open." So in the end he said that if you trust, you earn forgiveness."

The first time when I see coins here in America I remember the lost coin. This is surprising to me because some people in Africa don't know that Americans use coins. Some people in Africa think that Americans only use dollars.

In Swahili, we have a saying: Someone who walks and seeks nothing is better than someone who sits and seeks nothing.

The Golden Land

By Julia Sharo Phaw

Burma is fondly referred to as "The Golden Land" because of the country's beautiful golden pagodas. Today Burma is also known by a different name: Myanmar. Many Myanmar Royal Families donated gold to create the gold-plated pagodas all over the country. The pagodas were named "Shwe," meaning "golden," in our language.

Myanmar is an agricultural country. The main crop that farmers grow is rice. During harvesting time, we can see yellow and golden colors in the rice paddy fields. The golden paddy fields also represent Myanmar as the golden land.

Where is this Golden Land? It is located in Southeast Asia, bordering Bangladesh and India in the west and northwest area. The northern part of the country borders China. The east and southeast regions border Laos and Thailand. Myanmar has a long coastal area in the southern region.

The national capital city of Myanmar is Nay Pyi Taw. The government officially proclaimed the new city of Nay Pyi Taw, the capital of the country in 2006. The old capital city of Yangon (Rangoon) is the main seaport of the country. Many commercial businesses are located in Yangon.

The weather in Myanmar is divided into three seasons. They are summer, rain, and cold seasons. Summer starts from March to June. It is followed by the rainy monsoon season from July to October. Finally, between November to February is the cold season (winter). Depending on the seasons, the temperature can change from the north to the south. The northern regions have cooler climates and the delta and southern regions become hotter than the north.

In the summer, we have long holiday breaks in April. This is called the Thingyan Festival (Water Festival). This festival is celebrated during Myanmar's traditional ne year. People celebrate for 4 or 5 days. Thingyan represents the washing of the sins of the previous year and the preparation for the goodness for the coming new year. Following our traditional way, we sprinkle scented water to each other from silver bowls using Thabyay which are the leaves of a green tropical tree. The people from Myanmar believe that when they donate to the Thabyay in their pagoda, it can carry good luck to their lives. Many families hold a "Novice Ceremony" in the summer for their sons before they turn 20. They enter the monastery, and have their heads shaved. They live the life of a monk for one week. During that time, they offer a big donation and have a festive celebration. At the end of the ceremony, the novices ride elephants and horses in a parade. The elephant and horses are decorated in traditional clothing and jewelry.

During the monsoon season, farmers grow several species of crops like rice, wheat, beans and corn. Today they continue to use buffaloes or bulls to prepare the land. For this reason, the people from Myanmar are not willing to eat beef. Cows are important benefactors to the farmers. They provide a lot of manpower for agriculture like clearing weeds, plowing, maintaining and fertilizing the land.

The winter season is the time for harvest. So the farmers celebrate a thanksgiving ceremony. They donate their products to monasteries and churches. It is called the harvest festival. Farmers can harvest their crops plentifully. They invite their neighborhood to join their harvest festival. Normally, they treat their guests with the new crops they grow.

I love the culture and traditions from the Golden Land. Now that I am in the United States, I will never forget my family and my native country. I am so proud of where I came from.

Eid: A Special Day for Me

By Nooria FNU

Every year in the spring we have an important holiday called Eid. Eid happens after fasting for our religion for one month. We cannot eat or drink after sunrise and before sunset. This means that our only food is late at night or early in the morning. The time of EID changes every year, based on the Lunar Calendar. It is for three days after one month of fasting. It is more difficult to fast when it is hot outside, because we cannot drink water.

I celebrate Eid with my family and relatives in Afghanistan. Everyone in Afghanistan or people from Afghanistan living in other countries buys new clothing for the whole family. Women buy beautiful colorful dresses with pants called Shalwar. Men buy new leather shoes and long traditional shirt called Kurta that comes to their knees with a colorful vest. All of the clothing is colorful and beautiful.

When I was in Afghanistan, I cooked with my mom for Eid. We made Narij Pilau, which is a special rice dish with a type of bitter orange peel which has been sweetened (called Narij) and sliced almonds. It also has saffron and cardamom. We made beef or lamb with onions, oil, and garlic. We made homemade naan bread, homemade plain yogurt with mint, fresh vegetable salads and for dessert, sweet pudding with strawberries and sweet cakes or baklava.

We visit our families and close friends during the holiday. Children get money from their family and everyone gives small chocolates, boiled eggs or other snacks to children from the neighborhood who go knock on all the doors to say "Eid Mubarek", Happy Eid! Husbands give money to their wives.

Some people go to the parks and play games like volleyball or football, what you call soccer here. Other people go to the movie theater to watch special holiday movies.

Some people stay home to wait for their guests to come. People usually visit their relatives during Eid and if someone comes to your house, you have to have lot of good things to eat and drink for them. Sometimes we have 15 guests with all of their children. They can come any time during the holiday.

The next Eid will be on May 23rd and I am very excited because it is a special time. In America, it is not the same, but we still cook, celebrate and visit friends if our family is not here.

I miss having Eid with my family. Maybe you can come and eat delicious food at my house this year!

Proud to Serve the United States Army

By Sayed Abid

When I was in Afghanistan I worked with the United States Army as a translator. During that time, we faced many difficult situations. One day, my commander ordered us to search the village houses at midnight. He also said that the translators should stand in front of the soldiers during the searches. We translators were afraid that we may die. When midnight came we did not have a choice to refuse the commander's order. After searching three houses we found one group of militants that tried to attack us. Because of this attack, we lost many translators and other Afghan helpers.

After that, I decided that I needed to leave my job as a translator for the U.S. Army. I faced many threats because of my work with the U.S. army. They wanted information from me about U.S. strategies. I tried to petition the Afghan security departments, but unfortunately they never responded. I then escaped from Afghanistan and went to India. I had a very difficult time, financially, in India, so I had to come back to Afghanistan. I was scared to have to go back, but I had no choice. For two years, I hid my face so that no one would recognize me. Eventually, my neighbors warned me that people had asked about me. My fear greatly increased. I fled to Turkey because I knew I could not live like that.

When I arrived in Turkey, I found my U.S. commander.

I explained my story to him. He gave me a recommendation letter and I applied for a Special Immigrant Visa. After three years, the U.S. issued me this Visa because I had served with the U.S. Army. I am grateful to the U.S. government for the opportunity to be an American, and I am happy to finally feel safe.

You Aren't Where You Come From

By Destiny Hawes

All my life I have been surrounded by negative people and influences. I was raised by a drug addicted mother. Not the kind of mother a little girl should have, but a monster. I not only came from a drug addicted parent, but a drug addicted family. No matter where I turned I was completely surrounded by evil.

I grew up believing that drugs, alcohol, and child sex crimes were okay. At just nine years old I was molested for the first time by a close friend of the family. He was the last man I would have ever expected to hurt me. I remember coming home and telling my mother that I had been touched. She didn't believe me. When he was arrested, my mother was just mad she lost her babysitter.

After that, my mother made me commit a sex act for her drug habit. This abuse continued until I was 12 years old and deemed a ward of the state and placed in foster care. The rest of my teen years I was in and out of juvenile detention centers, lock down behavioral health care facilities and group homes for troubled teens. I became a foster child for at risk teens. At 16 years old, I was placed at the Discovery School of Virginia for girls, a wilderness work program in Dillwyn. At that point in life, I was completely against rules and structure of any kind. So you can imagine, I struggled big time at this work program. After the first three months of receiving consequences, I decided to stop bucking the system and work the program. After five months, I earned my crest an became trusted by the

37

staff. After six months, I received my first home visit. In November 2013 I went home for a week at Thanksgiving. Little did they know, I had not worked my program honestly, all I had worked was the system.

Once I got back home to Nelson County, I used my sister's cell phone and got in touch with a friend in Alexandria, and plotted my runaway plan. At 3 A.M., I was picked up and on the way to Alexandria. In the blink of an eye I went from being in a stable, structured environment, to a 17-year-old runaway, a long way from home.

Shortly after, I got pregnant with my baby girl. I spent the next year and a half on the run from Nelson County. My entire pregnancy I was a juvenile runaway. I turned 18 in May 2014 and I had my daughter in August 2014. Two weeks after she was born, we moved back home to Nelson County, so my daughter could meet her family.

That was the biggest mistake of my life. Three months after I moved back home, I was addicted to meth. It wasn't long after that I was doing drugs intravenously. I received my first felony charge as an adult, ended up on probation and have been in and out of jail.

As I write this, I am 23 and in the Albemarle Charlottesville Regional Jail on my second probation violation. Since I have been incarcerated I have gained quite a few things. I have reconnected with my daughter and started mending that relationship; I have started my GED classes, and I have graduated from my Moral Recognition Therapy class. These are all huge steps to my long term success.

I decide to write about "Where do you come from?" to let everyone know that no matter who you are and what negative things you come from, they don't make you. As long as you choose to change the cycle of where you came from, you can do better. Things you have gone through do not define you as a person. You aren't where you came from.

Work

Selfless

By Parinton Muangchantuek

I left my small country, Thailand, to become an au pair and live in the United States. When I decided to leave my home country to live here, I knew it would be hard. This new experience will challenge e, but I'm ready to let a big challenge into my life and let it happen. I knew my life would change completely.

Being an au pair is not like being a full-time nanny. It's about being completely selfless and doing things for the children. It's about having fun with them, smiling and watching them grow up. Sometimes it's not easy because of the different culture and place. The different language is especially hard and challenging. Many times I've been ready to give up but my soul says, "No! You have to keep going!!" or "You can do it! Fight for your dreams!" These feelings give me more power and energy to keep going. I'm very lucky to live with a lovely host family. They're nice and kind. They're open minded enough to listen and always help me deal with a problem or difficulty. Every time that I am met with a hard situation or I need help, they're happy to help me. In addition, every time I had some problem it was great to realize that I could find a solution if I had the patience to figure it out. No matter what the problem is, I am always grateful to my host family and my job makes me a better person. My motto is "be flexible, be nice, improve and be strong."

I still remember my first day here; how excited and nervous I felt. All the while learning something new. Every day I have silly questions to ask my host family or host kids and we laugh together. Sometimes my accent is hard to understand because the Thai accent is sometimes hard to understand. For example, Thai has separate letters for "R" and "I" sounds, but these are used interchangeably meaning, for example, that "very" is pronounced like "wely." Therefore, many times my host family and host kids guess what I said or what I meant, but it's a happy and funny time together.

The au pair program made me a different person. I have become more open, more confident and I believe in myself more than ever. It has been a wonderful and great opportunity to be an au pair. I am really thankful that my host family supports me and always loves me like a member of the family. Thank you so much for this experience. Without this program, I could not possibly have made all of the good memories that will make me happy when I think of the au pair experience.

"Heel" the World

By Soo Lim

When I just came to U.S.A., I led a meaningless life. My English was not good, and I was a little bit afraid to go out. I first lived in Baltimore. Baltimore had a high crime rate. Everyday there was a report on the news about different crimes.

One day, my friend proposed for me to go to a volunteer activity with her. So I decided to go with her to ODBEC (Our Daily Bread Employment Center). It is a Catholic charity. It's open 365 days a year.

At the beginning, actually I was fearful. Because there were many homeless people, drug addicts and criminals in the building we were serving. ODBEC served all the different people that needed help. They separated the criminals into the second floor. ODBEC wanted to reform them.

On the first day, before we worked, the staff said to us: "Breakfast is very important. It can change a person's day, moreover a person's life." We brought food to their tables just like in a restaurant. They didn't have to line up. They even could choose from a vegetarian menu.

I tried to give the good energy to them. I thought my smile and good attitude could make their day good. In the meantime, I felt full in my heart. Sometimes they requested to bring the 'heel'. At first, I didn't know what they meant. But I came to know it meant the crust end piece of a loaf of bread. I didn't know why they liked the 'heel'. But I came to understand them. The word 'heal' seemed to bring us closer together.

In conclusion, I enjoyed helping them. I had meaning in my life. They changed my life!

It has been more than a decade since this work experience. I raised a child and moved three times. My English is getting better. I'm also getting help from the TJACE program like I served for someone in Baltimore. They will experience us in their own ways, just as I had experienced us through the word 'heel'.

Do you know the song "Heal the World" by Michael Jackson? Perhaps many people will. I especially like it. Sometimes I hum that song. Sometimes I changed the word heal to "heel" the world' for me. Together we heal each other.

Balloon Volleyball

By Maria Harris

This is my story. My first job was in Chicago at a nursing home. It was about taking care of residents and dealing with different behaviors, so that can get kind of scary. So one day my boss told me I have to do activities with the residents. There were ten of them so I split them in half, five on one team and five on the other team, with a large net in between them. We played volleyball. That was fun and the residents had a lot of fun. I was not scared anymore and enjoyed myself as well. While working later they asked me if we can play the same game again. About two times a week, we set up volleyball to play with the residents. Before we even start to play, they fall asleep quickly. But as soon as they get hit by the balloon, they wake up. One day one of the residents, Paul, was playing in his wheelchair. He got up from the wheelchair and kicked the balloon. He was so happy.

Dreams Come True Never Give Up

By Edwin Qintanilla

15 years ago I came to New York to live with my uncle. Everything was perfect. I was making a lot of money. I worked every day 6am to 8pm. One day I met the mother of my beautiful baby. We decided to come to Virginia in 2011. The first three years was not good for me. What I was making here was a big difference from what I was making in New York. In 2014 my baby ws born. We were happy. Everything was good. But there was one problem. I was not making enough money—that was the big problem. One day we decided to separate. There were problems every day. One year later I met my current wife. She changed my life. In 2016 I started my own business in landscaping. My wife supported me to make my dreams come true. I remember one day I woke up earlier than usual because I had a lot of work on that day. I did my first three jobs. There was one more. I was feeling very tired, but at the same time I was happy because that was my last job for the day. When I got home my wife already made dinner so we can eat together. After that it was a good day.

Sorry, I Cannot Hear You

By Farida Laheb

In my second year of being in the United States, I decided to go back into the medical field, so I enrolled in a CNA class. After a while, I got a certificate.

Having an American certificate, I felt confident and thought about applying for a job even though my English was at a very low level. I applied for a CNA job at Martha Jefferson hospital and waited for their call. After one week, I received a call from the hospital, but it was not an invitation call. It was a real telephone interview.

The interviewer started to ask me questions. I could barely understand her. I asked her to speak more slowly and she started to speak slowly and clearly, but there was another problem. I was stuck—could not talk—I even forgot the simple words that I knew before. I realized that it was useless to continue, and I would not get the job, so I pretended that I didn't hear her and said, "Sorry, I can't hear you, the line is bad" and then dropped the telephone.

It was a bad and bitter experience for me and for a long time, I lost my confidence. After this experience, when I wanted to apply for a job, at first, I was interested to know if a phone interview was required. If it was, I declined.

Years passed.

Recently, I applied for a job and surprisingly, again, I was faced with a telephone interview. And this time, I did it successfully; they liked me and I got the job. Now I'm thinking, if I had never had that awful interview, I would never have worked so hard on my listening and speaking English skills.

2006, A Year to Remember

By Betty Mkungusi

In the year 2006, I had a beautiful and popular restaurant in Nairobi Kenya. One morning on the 20th June 2006, life changed for me. The restaurant got burned to ashes as I watched helplessly. The next day I had no job to go to. My world had crumbled. Tears could not help. Days, weeks and years passed. I did not have a job. My car was repossessed. I could not afford anything. Life was unbearable.

My daughter, who was living in the US, had dropped out of school. She started working to sustain us. I developed blood pressure and diabetes. My friends in Kenya advised I come to the US to be close to my daughter. I arrived here in December, 2010. I got a job of babysitting which I did for five years with three different families who were all wonderful people. They understood me. I remain grateful to them, and they are like family to me now. Later I got a job which I worked for three years.

In the year Jan 2018, I fell while working on icy snow and injured my back. I was in and out of hospital the whole of that year. In November that year I was stopped from working from work because of my injury. My world turned round again because it meant I did not have insurance for my needs.

Through 2019, it wasn't easy getting a job because of the injury. I have now enrolled with computer classes at Adult Learning Center to be able to get a job that befits my injury. I still have hope and trust that all will be well.

I Want to Be a Good Hair Stylist

By Zahra Khaveri

My name is Zahra Khaveri. I work in a beauty salon that is called Moxie. The owners are Todd and Michael. I love my work because I have a good boss. Everybody is happy in the salon because we are learning new things like, how to color hair and about different ways to cut and blow dry hair. My work has a good future for me. The work is about making people's face and hair more beautiful. It has different challenges. People have different hair. We need to learn about many kinds of shampoos and conditioners and which ones are most suitable for each type of hair. Some people want to stand out from everybody else. They want to change the appearance of their hair and face with makeup and a haircut. I can help people feel better about themselves. I want to be a good hair stylist.

Education

Old Pillow in Borrowed Beds: What Education Became to Me

By Xueping Wang

Education has become a passion for me. Never does it stop. People acquire an education throughout their lives. It makes people understand responsibility. It teaches people obligation to five to the world around them through sharing and learning.

When I moved to the United States, I closed myself off to the room in the apartment I rented and the barber chair I worked from at Chung's Barbershop. My heart closed in missing home near inner Mongolia. The rolling piedmont of central Virginia was peopled with strangers who spoke a different language and had unfamiliar ways than Chinese. I felt a foreigner for not having had a complete education. I felt sad in not being able to talk with them. English was too hard for a farmer's son.

Later, a lack of education led me to feel like I had lost myself under the foothills of Monticello. I was out of step with the world changing. Loneliness made me realize I needed to find myself, accept hardship and challenge my predicament. Leaned up against an old pillow in borrowed beds, I felt isolated. Americans spoke to me, but I could not understand their words. I asked myself "How could I be a good barber if I did not speak English in the United States?"

With no choice and wanting to do the best job I could, I would have to make new friends, learn English and American culture. The problem was I did not know how since I had only reached a 9th grade education back in Chins. One day a customer told me about the Charlottesville Literacy Center. In August 2014, I began my education again long past the days when I was a teenage boy in Lian Feng Cun.

Despite working six days a week and attending church twice, I began meeting a tutor once a week for two hours. I began to interact with Americans through meeting my tutors—Robert, Sam, Suzanne and Erin. First, I worked on conversational English so that I could speak to my customers and make American friends. After three years I switched to learn reading and writing in English.

Gradually, my coworkers realized I had changed. Because my English pronunciation improved so much, I could communicate with customers. Quickly I encouraged them to do the same by sharing how education can change our lives for the better. Like me when I felt isolated leaning up against old pillows of borrowed bed, my coworkers worried they could not learn to speak English. Fortunately, I convinced some of them to attend tutoring at the Literacy Volunteers Center. Despite working every day, they have continued to study until now.

Beside learning to speak, read and write English, I have learned how important it is to study the culture and history of my new home in Charlottesville. Soon I would learn how Virginia was one of the original thirteen colonies. A customer and good friend began to teach me about the Constitution with its separation of power and checks and balances. Far from isolated, I learned how Thomas Jefferson had aided America to become the greatest example of democracy in world history.

Education allowed me to grow in my new home. New lessons open up to me as endless as the un-counted times one of America's greatest minds looked out from Monticello. Now, I can communicate well with many Americans. I have made lifelong friends with them. We share our life experiences together with me teaching them of Chinese culture. I am pleased to share with my new friends and help my coworkers learn English and American culture.

I left behind old pillows of borrowed beds of my past loneliness as a foreigner in my new home in Virginia. Reading, writing and speaking English taught me how education changes each of our lives for the better.

Believe in Yourself

By Seyed Ali Hashemi

Have you ever been told by everybody, including your closest friends that you can't do something? Maybe you even start to panic and believe they are right! I want to tell you my experience about how people's negative thoughts affected me.

I was not originally from Turkey. I came into the country when I was eleven. So when I was in high school in Turkey, my friends did not believe I could pass the exam and get into a university. You had to take an exam, and your score would determine if you could attend a university or not. No one thought I could do well on the exam.

Many reasons affected how successful you can be, such as, your school, your teachers or even where you lived. My school was one of the worst schools in town. The students were constantly fighting and yelling. It was a terrible atmosphere and it was impossible to learn anything there. The teachers were not able to teach. There was always a fight somewhere or some other violence at the school. The principal and teachers couldn't do anything.

My friends were telling me that it was impossible to pass the test for a foreign student like me. I started to think that maybe they were right! I started to panic and had nightmares in my dream. I felt so bad about myself. It was scary to think about failing and not having a future. Sometimes, I thought about giving up too, and didn't bother myself too much. I was feeling a lot of pressure in that time, and to be honest, most of the time. I couldn't handle it.

I didn't want to do anything and I wanted to be alone. Sometimes I stopped studying for a while because everybody was telling me Id fail. Then I started to think of my family and what they went through to get me here. I started to feel guilty, and started to study again. I hadn't any other choice. I wasn't from a rich family. I was a refugee and hadn't enough money to start a business. So I kept studying and they kept telling me "you can't" louder every day!

Then the exam day came, and I took it. I had some mistakes, but I finally did it. Two months later the university published the matching board online. I saw my name matched with the medical school. I was shocked. Nobody was there to celebrate with me. I started thinking back to those days that everybody was telling me "you can't." After that I made some changes inside me, that no one can tell me who I am and what I am capable of. I experienced many bad days but they gave me a big lesson. Always do your best and you can succeed.

The Power of Your Dreams

By Maria Helena Reino Matta

Who doesn't want to make their dreams come true? I do and I am sure you do, too. Everybody has dreams and goals and everybody is able to make them possible. Is that hard? Mmmm, I don't know. I guess that depends on you and how hard you work for them.

6 years ago, In Bogotá, Colombia, there was a 15-year-old girl, (Yes, that's me). I was in my last year of high school, looking for different careers and colleges, all of them super expensive. My parents didn't tell me anything, but inside I knew that they were not able to pay for my college. However, I had a dream and I really wanted to make it come true. One day in March, I was watching TV with my mom and the commercial came out (The ones that are really boring and no one wants to watch). For the first time I was paying attention to them. It was a great choice, because one of them was talking about scholarships that the government was planning to give to the best students in the country. Yay, my mom, my grandmother, my father and my siblings, were so excited. Of course, it is an awesome opportunity. But wait, one of the requirements was to score really high in the ICFES, this is an important test that all the students take in Co-

lombia in their last year of High school to determinate readiness for College. Am I able to do that? That was my first question. Of course, I am. And in that moment the best year of my life started. Every day, I was awake at 5 in the morning and I went to sleep at 11 at night. I had my school, my hobbies, my basketball team, my homework, my lessons for the test and my home responsibilities: a crazy life for a 15 years old right?

The time was running and the day of the test arrived. There was a lot of pressure, but at the same time a lot of trust in myself and in God. The day was done, I was done. The next step? Wait until the scores were ready.

Here it comes the best part of the story. October 10. My dad's birthday and guess what? The same day when scores were published. An excellent present for my dad or the biggest disappointment. I only remember all my family around me in the table. I was with my phone in my hands, waiting with my eyes closed and the time came, I got the score, I really did it! The best day in my life!

6 years later, here we are. I am an Environmental Engineer. I am so proud of myself. I did excellent work with my family and friend`s support, but especially, I thank God. Do I have more dreams? Of course, I do. I am here in a different country, learning a new language. Let's see what is the end of this story.

Learning to Fly in America

By Marcela Cruz

I want to be a flight attendant in Brazil, but I need to know English. All flight attendants in Brazil need to learn English. The airlines expect a high level of English and coming to the United States would help. I knew that being a nanny would be a good way to learn and I have always loved kids. I have five younger brothers, and three young nieces. I always helped take care of them when I was in Brazil. I also volunteered at the orphanage. I would play games inside with them and go out to the playground. We would play basketball, volleyball, and soccer. I was scared on my first day of work in the United States because the English I learned in Brazil was very different. I was afraid I would not be able to communicate with the family.

I was lucky because the family was very understanding and helped me learn quickly. Although I knew how to take care of my family and the orphans in Brazil, the food and culture in the United States is very different. I needed to learn what American kids enjoy eating and drinking. I realized that people eat meals at very different times in the United States and I needed to adjust. I talked to the family and quickly learned what they enjoyed eating and doing during the day. That first day I made them quesadillas and tacos because they told me they enjoy Mexican food. Since then, I have shared Brazilian food with the family, which they enjoyed.

The kids here do the same activities as the kids in

Brazil. On the first day, I took them to the playground and we played outside. There were plenty of differences but the similarities between my family and this new one made my work easier. The first day was very difficult but I was excited. I was happy to meet the family and have the opportunity to learn English. The family was helping me achieve my dream.

Going to School: A Funny Story

By Khatima Yari

My story from Tuesday, November, 5th:

I came to class at the Adult Learning Center.

After class, I went to The Jefferson School.

I looked for my teacher, Sunny, inside the room. And she was not there.

I asked at the front desk. "Hi Maureen, is Sunny here?"

"She was, I don't know."

"OK. Thank you."

Oh, I needed to call her and we talked on the phone.

She said "I am sorry. I sent a message for you last minute. I have a bad cold, and see you next week."

That was my fault. I didn't check my phone because she sent the message in the morning at 8:55. Oh, I needed to call the Jaunt service to cancel it.

I needed to go to the CAT bus and walked to the bus stop, then looked inside my backpack. Oh, no, I forgot my wallet today! I had no bus pass, no money, and I sent a message for my nephew. "Are you working today?", and he was. "Yes, I am at work now."

I called for my friend. She didn't answer.

I needed to go in the Afghan grocery. I asked the manager "Can you give me a dollar for the bus? I forgot my wallet today." And he said "Sure."

I took it and went to the bus stop. I went inside the bus and looked at the pay machine. It was closed because it was Election Day.

I got home and ate some food and drank tea. Then I started to write this story.

Sometimes things happen, and they are little funny.

Becoming a Doctor in Kazakhstan

By Aimal Osmani

I am from Afghanistan and I am a doctor. I graduated from medical school in Kazakhstan in the city of Almaty in 2019. I finished school in Afghanistan in 2010. In 2011, I want to Kazakhstan and in 2012, I started medical school Asfandyarov Kazakh National Medical University. In First year I did not understand Russian and I used to always translate. In second and third year, I spoke and understand very well. In 2017, I graduated from General Medical School and also started internship in general surgery at hospital number seven in Almaty city. I finished the internship in 2019.

When I was in eighth grade, I realized I loved science and medicine. I decided I wanted to be a doctor because I wanted to help people. I was good at understanding mathematics, physics, chemistry and biology. It is very hard to become a doctor in Afghanistan, but many hard working students had the dream to become one. I worked very hard and I was able to start medical school in Afghanistan. I started my first semester, but then I passed my exams and I got a scholarship to go to medical school in Kazakhstan. 2,000 students take this exam, but only 100 students get the scholarship to go. I did not have any family in Kazakhstan, so I had to go there by myself in 2011 and I was only 19 years old. I lived in student housing, we call it a hostel there, and I had to do everything by myself. I did not even know their language, so I had to teach myself Russian. For six days of the week, I would study Russian to get better. From nine in the morning to three in the afternoon, I went to school for one semester. I had to cook, clean, and I worked like a wife. I made friends who were also from Afghanistan, we were all able to start school together. But when I started school, I had to live with two people I did not know. Most students came from Loger and Kabul, my roommates were from Loger. I lived with one of them for eight years, and I still talk to them sometimes.

I did five years of general medicine and two years of an internship where we actually practiced like doctors. When I first started, I used to get lower grades because I didn't understand the language. Then in the later years, my grades were a lot higher. I hope one day to become a plastic surgeon, but that is difficult to do in the United States. Two months ago, I came to the United States when I got married. Now, I am studying English and I am working at Giant Foods in pick-up. But I am working so that one day I can go back to medicine, so I am studying the USMLE books and listening to lectures to prepare for my exam. I hope to finish my dream of becoming a plastic surgeon one day soon.

Education Is Important

By Tajalla Babakerkheil

Education is essential part of our life. There is a big difference between educated and uneducated people. As an uneducated person, they can see the world around, but they cannot read the words on the page. They are blind to all the word written words. Education opens their eyes to see new opportunities, new ways of thinking and knowledge of all things. We cannot ignore the importance of education in our life at any cost. The first purpose of getting good education is being good citizen and then being successful in the future. We are uncomplicated without education because education makes us thinker and correct decision maker. We can get a better job in the future with a good education and we will develop our country and communities. I have lived in the U.S. since 2018 and I am graduated from high school in my country. When I was in my country I could not speak English. In 2018 I came to the U.S. After three months I started to speak English because I finished 12th grade in my country.

It is a bit easier for me to learn a new language. I have a friend from my country who has never been to school in our country. She has been living in the U.S. for four years and she still cannot speak English because she has never been to school. I always encourage her to go to school and I am helping her to learn English, but it is very hard for her.

The biggest and most valuable lesson that I have learned is the importance of education.

My English Journey

By Dehui "Gary" Geng

I began to learn English when I was in middle school, just like other Chinese students in my generation. To me, it was a brand new thing at that time. The feeling of freshness drove me forward. I learned simple grammar and memorized new words and English articles. Easy method, and I earned good English test scores. I thought learning English is just about memorizing new words.

In high school, to me, English was an important subject which determined if I could go to a good university or not. Just memorizing words seemed not to work very well. I could not understand long sentences. I talked with my tutor and analyzed my approach to learning English by myself. Maybe I should focus on grammar. I did so and it worked very well. I received high scores again. I thought English learning is just about memorizing plus grammar.

I didn't have much learning pressure in university. But we had a CET test which means College English Test. I can get an English CET certificate if I pass the test. The certificate would be very useful for finding a good job after graduation. To me, English is a bridge to future career. I used what I had learned, but did really poorly in the listening part of the test. Until then, I knew English is not just about reading and writing, but also listening. So I spent time listening to English materials, like English news. I persisted and got the certificate.

I actually had realized the importance of speaking during the same time I realized listening was important. But I was stubborn to think that if I did well in reading, writing, and listening then I will surely do very well in speaking. Due to working reasons, I had some opportunities to talk with clients from other countries. But I found that I can't even speak a whole sentence smoothly. My speaking needed practice.

Now, I have been in the US for more than one year. And I met many native teachers and friends who are also trying to learn English. They helped me a lot and I was very encouraged. I have been used to looking up materials through the internet using English. I keep learning from my teachers here. I keep speaking English with friends from all over the world. I am trying to think about every sentence in English. I save English related pictures and videos on my phone and clarify them. Now there are more than ten thousand pictures and videos on my phone. One year is not long, but I have made a big improvement. Two month ago, I took the IELTS test and reached the standard for applying for my master degree in English speaking countries. One year is not long, but I got to many new cultures and made lots of friends all over the world. One year is not long, but I broadened my horizon and opened my mind. Suddenly, I found that to me, learning English has become a part of my life.

One language sets you in a corridor for life. Two languages open every door along the way. When people are trying to learn new languages. They might feel the more they learn the harder it will be. I know the journey to learning English is not easy, but the scenery along the journey is beautiful. Let's keep going.

Made in the USA
Columbia, SC
11 March 2020